JUST A
GIRL WHO
LOVES JESUS
& DANCING

JUST A GIRL WHO LOVES JESUS & DANCING

JUST A
GIRL WHO
LOVES JESUS
& DANCING

JUST A GIRL WHO LOVES JESUS & DANCING

JUST A GIRL WHO LOVES JESUS & DANCING

JUST A GIRL WHO LOVES JESUS & DANCING

www.ingramcontent.com/pod-product-compliance
Lightning Source LLC
LaVergne TN
LVHW060201080526
838202LV00052B/4180